Quantum Foam

poems of random fluctuations

Stephen Hegarty

BookLeaf Publishing

India | USA | UK

Made with ❤ on the BookLeaf Publishing Platform
www.bookleafpub.in
www.bookleafpub.com

Dedication

*To the memory of Dodo and
Millie from Malden
who let me be peculiar.*

Preface

"The conception of the objective reality of the elementary particles has thus evaporated in a curious way, not into the fog of some new, obscure, or not yet understood reality concept, but into the transparent clarity of a mathematics that represents no longer the behavior of the elementary particles but rather our knowledge of this behavior."

--Werner Heisenberg, *The Representation of Nature in Contemporary Physics*, 1958

Acknowledgements

I blame no one, I won't let myself off the hook. Self-inflicted wounds, all of it. I'm just trying to understand why.

1. Entanglement

When particles interact
    physically
    and then become separated
    they remain
entangled,
inextricably connected,
communicating,
    spooky action at a distance.
Their shared state
is indefinite
    until measured.

How to characterize
    a part of reality
    of which one has
    no
    direct sensory experience?
In fact, bodies could be
almost anywhere
    until you look for them.

Knowing where they are
    exactly
    requires infinite energy

And that's

    impossible.

2. Dark matter

is only a name
for what we do not
understand
clearly enough to give
another name

so out of reach
all we can do is
    think about it

3. Event horizon

In layman's terms is it defined as
"the point of no return,"
    the point at which the
    gravitational pull
    becomes so great
    as to make
escape
    impossible.

From the observer's side
    any object
    approaching
 the horizon appears
    to slow down.

The traveling object
    experiences no
    strange effects.

All paths that light takes are
warped.

Light from some events
    never

intersects

    the observer's worldline.

Events are unobservable

and can not

affect

an outside observer.

Attempting to make an object

    near the horizon

    remain stationary

    requires a force whose magnitude

increases

unbounded

becoming

infinite.

4. Saturn V

The Apollo astronauts trained
for every eventuality.

The one thing
they could not train for

was the dynamics
of a Saturn V liftoff.

It was
violent.

There were wrenched
all over

like a rabbit
in the jaws of a whippet.

They couldn't hear themselves

think.

5. Reentry

is thankfully buffered
four hour...drive...from the airport

a singular moment
out of time collapses
back into real world

the pitch and yaw
shuttling
between worlds

sometimes invigorating
sometimes exhausting

so simple, so prodigious
it happens so fast then
it happens
forever
live in memory of vapor

    i don't know what
    that arrangement was
    i could never tell
    like you could

when, where i will see you
try to escape

coffee and a cigarette
you had a hell of a time

so be gentle on yourself

friend, lover
smitten, blissful denial
exhilarated, racing

    all the while

    simulacra to sustain
    webs to weave

i know now which is which
and what angle i ought
to look at it from

even ephemera leave stains

    vows avowed
raw and forsworn

helpmeet, stranger
wasted, suboptimal grief
broken, hollow

all the while

bruises to indulge
scabs to pick

a violent gash i can't be arsed to treat

there's a simple
fix for all this

    keeping a candle lit
a fucking metaphor, right?

empty your pockets
get right with jesus

make time, die trying
look alive, don't listen

whatever works

to keep

what?

who?

from shattering
into so many

ugly
shards

6. Decoherence

Anyone who says they understand is lying.
All their eigenstates, one-half spins, wave function
collapses, universes running in reverse
dismal science is trying my every last nerve.
I mean, 26 dimensions, most so profoundly
hidden they'll never be encountered? Political
scientists with slide rules measuring human behavior.
Fuck me.
I grant certainty is a figment; I concede we live in a
reality
of possibilities and potentialities, not a fortress of things
and facts.
Totally down with that; it's liberating.

But. Things never need defending
facts are drowning and we can't find a life jacket.
Nothing is provable and everything is debatable.
Experience is a liar, sapience is a myth.
All the verities at the root of any
collective solidarity we've eked out
are mere concoctions and truther now
means fabulist and every day is the stupidest day ever.

Now. I'm not going to go all three-body here

tinfoil hat purity of essence physics doesn't exist
anymore.
I ought to be a fearless turkey pushing the envelope.
Seems perverse, given we're drowning in data
about ourselves, each other, completely meaningless shit.
But. Essential information is an endangered species,
we have so little to slough off into the aether.
Every system not perfectly, absolutely isolated
bleeding coherence over time is the bedrock one and all
wobble upon.

The only surety is uncertainty. I say again:
I embrace it, being unsure is my modus operandi.
So QED is a marvel and a terrific success,
pretty weak sauce for distilling hopes and dreams.
The God particle is essential, and decays instantaneously
upon creation,
a leaky vessel.

How do I fill all the holes in me in the void
with no certain thing? Give me just one enduring dingus.
Some terrible beauty, a beneficent overlord, that fine
madness,
the corruption of my body for the deliverance of my
soul.
Just as well to play dice with the devil.

Something, anything. Almost.

7. Dirac equation

I have trouble with
this balancing on the
dizzying precipice
between genius and madness.

I don't know what I knew before.

8. Skydiving on Venus

i don't belong in this place,
nothing grows in the right direction.

is that?
are the mountaintops glistening
with snowshine in this
vision of hell?

can't be because,
well, physics.
but no matter.
i'm negotiating more pressing concerns.

(lol! "pressing concerns"! hurtling
through opaque clouds of sulfuric acid
toward a surface oppressed by
ninety two atmospheres.
see what i did there?)

venera13 gave us the first
color photo of the surface.
and lasted all of 127 minutes.
jesus, less than an hour and a half.

what particular delusion among
the myriad knocking around my skull
gave me to believe
i was stronger than
an 800 kilogram state-of-the-art
hermetically sealed pressure capsule.

well cutting-edge for the ossifying
USSR in 1981, so. maybe.

a lump of sugar soaked in
sulfuric acid blooms

into a grotesque gob
of sludgy cremated remains.

eh, here goes.

9. Permission to abort, denied

a five hour drive slogs
into seven, struggle session
at the rest stop

we're worried, you're being erratic

waze fucks you up in circles
in the place you grew up,
where the streets no longer make sense

sideswipe a parked car, rip
off the mirror
don't fucking stop

boys in the back seat
wondering, maybe
scared, almost certainly

how fucked up is dad?

ribbons of police tape
wrapping the parking lot, warning
this place is impossible to reach,

maybe even dangerous?

in through the out door
two seedy dudes in a dingy back hall
mirrored sunglasses, backwards sox caps
greasy slices on a shredded fake leather couch

the clincher, an emptyish dive bar separating
the back entrance from the front desk
with a goddamn hippie band setting up
the drinks are practically screaming, c'mon just a couple

every direction is down here,
to see family on the day
it got real

"system's broke"
get in line
more time to catastrophize

my boys, blameless, coerced into
roles in my farcical passion play

hillary i think? perky, funny, apologetic
for...being decent and kind?
blink hard, hysterical double take
cardboard cutout of a cartoon trying

everyone's last nerve

dipshit she's sorry for
the stink rising off you
flop sweat, fumes, dread
sloughing the residue of this terrible world

lake quannapowitt, freckled, glistening
from snug, not untidy room 214
depthless calm to an
unquiet mind

this annual pilgrimage, ever joyful
their second favorite after christmas
stumblebums joyfully making a shambles of a scramble
charity tournament to honor the memory
of everyone's beloved, an angel taken too soon

the gauntlet passed but skulking
here now on inadequate beds
they are tentative, wary
diverted by sportscenter
squinting sideways at the

tensed back of the
opaque form still, floundering
at the window masking

turmoil with the bogus
tranquility of a glorified puddle
a scared
little boy plonked into
dad's chuck taylors

thirsty, parched even, bone-dry
hungry only for the flow state
the boys can tell somehow but
they need food, not your noisome remedy
our own greasy slices from
grimy wakefield house of pizza
supper muted but pretty fucking tasty

the low thrum of the
hippie band breaks the
mood such as it is and i
hurt for a cigarette

take the stairs, through the
now buzzing bar clenched
teeth balled fists laser focus
on the back door to the lake

the hippie band is really
just regulars, friends neighbors trying
to make a joyful noise together

chainsmoke for twenty or so thinking
hoping pleading
golf cousins aunties and
grammy in her glorious nuttiness
will shift the frame for the boys
for me
for the boys sure doubtful
for me you wouldn't believe
the shitty thoughts i think

man, all is forgiven...
without prejudice

you can't go home again
is bullshit people
do it all the time
it's never what
you want but
maybe it's all
you need

august 1, 2019

10. one revolution

everything's changed and
nothing is different
got here one
day at a time
so does
everyone else
all the tired
platitudes are true
i remembered in passing
almost by accident
the same washed out vacant
february morning not
cold enough stormy enough
anything enough
to be interesting
disease disorder moral turpitude
who the fuck cares
toxic inside and out is
all that figures
one revolution
later older wiser
if fatuous navel gazing coupled
with precocious decrepitude
is your idea of wisdom

congratulations for what
not dying
i did fuck all
except
stumble into the
preposterous fortune of not utterly alienating
one ardent exceptional woman
one revolution
later older feebler

addict honest
at the core
it's terrifying
all the things
i broke
are still broken

11. 8 stone

"So here they wait, untouched, alone,
These quiet witnesses—eight stone."
--Write a poem called 8 stone, ChatGPT, 2025

lovely, elegiac even
rubbish

the machine spits out
what you don't
even know you want

i want all of it
a bottle of this
a bag of that whatever you got
to transport me to the zone
spinning in the flow state
for decades insensate
for months drowning

i didn't know
i wanted 8 stone brittle
dulled bewildered crippled

you don't always get what you want

everything everything
tells me we are social
creatures the neuroscience
i read the depression swash
i wallow in the people
i love

our brains don't work
right in isolation we're
fundamentally wired wired!
to interact with
other beings
another damn machine

still: lash me to a mast
any sturdy fucking thing
keep me apart

and we'll see

12. Internal model

Everyone is living
one half second
in the past in
a beautifully rendered
simulation.

Snuggled in the womb
slippage transpired mispairing ensued.
Or something.
Maybe, it was losing eyeless
shabby Petey at
Canobie Lake Park, abandoned.
In any event mine's broken, stubbornly
sticking one
half life
in the past.

Chimeras and phantasms
congeal in the gutter
under a crapulous fog.
The gutter swells
to a trench, hollows
deepens to a pit,
the groundwork is

in smithereens.
The fog putrefies
to a noisome miasma.

All I get is disbelieving blinks
when I insist the pit is real
i'm being buried alive
and just digging digging.
I think they think
I'm just not trying.
So I quit even bothering.

Putting up with
this shit, ain't I.
Another day another day
not another day.
I am trying.

You're not you when you're asleep

13. Brown study

Lack of company will do it, they say
Intense reflection, distraction,
befuddlement also. No valence
is attached, it seems: maximum absorption
in sorting a problem, melancholic rumination,
sheer absent-mindedness all count.

Whatever its contours,
manifestations it is
fundamentally a temporary condition.
One falls in, and hours days
later emerges on the other side
better? wiser? just sadder?
Who knows.

There's no place like home.

14. Yersinia pestis

Everyone blames the rats, as if
they did it on purpose just
to make us mad with revulsion, also
dead in the millions.
They died too, in their silent, solitary agony
only then did the infernal fleas
forsake them to sow
their cursed seed.

Still we hate, even torture
in the name of progress,
pitiless hysterical outrage against the muroids.
But only the big ones.
The little ones are cute.

15. Around 1800 hours, 22 October, 4004 BCE

*"Which beginning of time, according to our Chronologie,
fell upon the entrance of the night before the twenty
third day of Octob, in the year of the Julian Calendar,
710."*
*--James Ussher, Archbishop of Armagh and Primate of
All Ireland, The Annals of the World, 1658*

there you have it, in the beginning
was a fairy tale and
the hokum has only
gone forth and multiplied
ever since.

this guy who wanted me to call him slick
took me on a field trip
live oaks, unmarked mailboxes, dirt roads to
a hole in the wall
somewhere in the vicinity of bon secour
freshest shrimp on the gulf coast,
i couldn't eat anyway.
standard southern bonhomie
where y'all from? ha ha all that
snow way up near tennessee

murky squinting incomprehension
at me: where now?

around fourteen billion years, or
sure, i'll grant it, six thousand in your fable
of the beginning. whatever. i am where
i am and you're where you are
we all of us sleep under different stars.

16. 47 U.S.C. §230

rage, go on, rage
against the dying of the light.
resist, blinkered, ridicule
the luminous darkness.
strings being pulled,
they get all the calls it's fixed,
a cabal calling the shots,
things fall apart, fume.
back and to the left.
you'd commit genocide but
your grades weren't good enough.
if you're not at the table
you're on the menu.
if you're not paying for the product,
you are the product.
the best defense against
propaganda is more propaganda
precious attention commodified
about a dozen insidious gray
oligarchs enslave us.
mission accomplished?

17. Вместо приписки

"Years ago I was ambitious.
But now it is clear that nothing will happen.
All those poems that made me soar along a foot
from the ground are not so much forgotten as never
read in the first place. They rolled like moons
of light into a puddle and were drowned. Not even
the puddle can be located now. Yet I am encouraged
by the way you hanged yourself, telling me that
such things don't matter."
--Jim Harrison, Letters to Yesenin

a need wells to add a postscript, but what
anything would do violence and
that's probably the point

building is better but breaking is easy and
oftentimes i can't tell which is what.

i don't know what's wrong with me but
i wish

it was something else

18. The magnetic woodpecker will set me free

"I think I'll throw it all away
I think I'll throw it all away
And if dreams come back to me
I'll pretend that I don't see
I'll just cover my eyes instead

It'll surely come
It'll surely come
Here it comes again"
—Yo La Tengo, The Ballad of Red Buckets

I.
there wasn't a word for it
for a long time, at least one that I knew
it wasn't even a thing. we had our folkways
and plenty of ways to misname it—moody
was always a favorite, also sulky, sullen
all a bit crude, still i was handled with kid gloves
'cause, y'know, the boy is sensitive.

i put a date on it now, have to
so the professionals can tick a box:
sixteen, also had my first eleven

34

drinks too many. what a coincidence.
but the ogre like as not was there
at inception, I can invent
memories of the lonely pall.

sixteen is not completely arbitrary,
a boundary after which my oddity
didn't need to be imagined. Submitted
for your consideration: a dorm room, hanover
spring 1986 six (or five?) friends a collective
via captivation by the russian language and
maybe just raw attraction. all but one devised
a parlor game; let the chatter wither
each by each til nothing, just fidgeting in silence.
let's see how long it takes him to disturb
the stillness, awkward for them checking
the stopwatch. He never did.
I had nothing to say.

years, lives later learning
the nickname one the wisest of the collective
invented: dr. jekyll & mr. hegarty.
More than clever, a shame I was oblivious
in the moment it might have helped. Doubtful,
but at least it would've been a good laugh.

II.

still don't have a word for it, willful
ignorance, denial even as it
oppresses, warps, splits me—
a simple avatar of gothic horror.
wicked smart, amusing, curious
movie star handsome (says uncle tim)
wicked quiet, aloof, curious
illiterate emotional hobo (whispers everyone i'm sure)
i've lived a million lives in my head and remain
inexperienced, unprepared for what comes next.
fireworks, rug burns, fervent post-its,
cruel in ending, inconstant in beginning
never never land.
surely the monomaniac scribbles and doodles flailing for
the perfect—fuck good enough—variation of that score
are long ago dulled, wearisome.
so. content to present, for your consideration:
another dorm room, cambridge alone now
spent, dead of night march 4, 1989.
insistent bang banging finally
shatters the spell clayit's
yourdadheartattackambulancehosp...how is

he didn't make it.

that's it.

a useless fancy phone that never rang
gelid, rigid by the time I got there
a half-life later kneeling, critical to rise, endure
swoon, stumble, stayed (uncle pat this time).

and that's it.

locked in an inner coffin, let it rot
do go fucking near it.

III.
the ink spilled on what happiness is
would choke a horse, most of it worth less than
the shit the pony leaves in its wake.
happiness is a choice rankles especially.
someone got close, beg pardon
I don't remember who: happiness is not a state
to arrive at, but a manner of traveling.

i rode that train for a good long while
the love of my life bought my ticket
beans and rice or lamb chops same same
omg these miraculous miniature beings
the scif in foggy bottom, braking for a herd of javelinas
the inner sanctum of gūr-e amīr, drunken klobása at 2am
a belated proper diamond, all that baseball
onion skin love letters, drinks in kerrytown

delight upon blessing in a mist barely clocked

i wasn't doing it right even so
muscling through the bounding quagmire
eggshells and fault lines
always thirsty never sated until
one of the cracks, meticulously untended
so long bursts sobbing shaking everything
a dead end, broken thoughts i can't fix
she dropped everything to hold me,
soothe and let her love open the door

but it was the beginning of the end

IV.
there's still no word, at least one i've learned
but i confuse: the beast has many names
and still the evidence is like trying to hold water
in your fist as if aspirin deficiency caused my headache
the word i lack is for the bottom below the bottom
and the liminal abysm under that
if you give it a name it becomes a thing maybe
that helps others believe it's real i've been there
felt its hopeless death stare unwittingly wanting
to return to dust
and i don't give a fuck if
you think i'm mental for believing i've been there

this song is already too fucking long so
no details in this verse they're
all too sickening and shameful anyway
i fall back on a song lyric somehow forgotten
yet there on a loop my personal cosmic background
radiation
my life's a mess, i wait for you to pass
i stand here at the bar, i hold an empty glass

recovered, just barely and unwilling
the grace of that exceptional woman again
recovering in fits, the beast ever present sometimes
dormant sometimes overpowering
the meds, the talk, the every damn thing
i'm counseled to do

the magnetic woodpecker will set me free.

if not, then what

19. the things that i lost here

the doors that keep closing
all the hands i let go of
the glare where i forgot her
all that sourmash just for nothing

the purpose i never fulfilled
sounds from a house, a hundred dead pumpkins
the life i was dreaming, a crayon for breaking
every trivial foible i shouldn't have tried to hide

a broken in blue glove, shoulders to stand on
eating hotdogs with a knife and fork
small beer, a riddle to sing along to
the view between spaces, attending not belonging

sand fleas at twilight, the tank I left empty
an enduring odyssey, rockets and candlepins
thirty two inches of snow, 110 in the shade
the tang of grace, delight and folly, and my rage in
firelight

a shoehorn with teeth, a fire in the shed,
tamales at christmas, endless cats and confederate dogs
rubbing out puddles of wax, three stooges all growed up

the jokes that aren't funny anymore

and never really were.

i remember now: five bucks on
what a wonderful world or
we'll meet again. you were guessing.
i always knew.

20. Talking Points for Discussion with the Grandchildren

- I sleep like a medieval peasant, in two shifts, three to fours each on a good night. In the interval, I read, paint, sometimes even cook. I'm embarrassed by this, I think, so I don't tell people. Discuss: What are the plusses and minuses of this sleep pattern?

- I own a guitar and a banjo and can't play more than a couple chords on either. They stare at me in silent rebuke from their stands in the corner, still I love holding, simply looking at them. Not learning to play an instrument, or even just singing and singing, even though I'm not good at it, is a hole in my life. Discuss: Why does practice suck so bad, and why is it so essential?

- There is a curious insistent strain in my self-concept that convinces me over and over again that what I am, really, is a hall of fame caliber baseball player trapped in the existence of an ineffectual dilettante.

Discuss: What was wrong with PeePaw?

- I never grieved my father properly. Put it all in a box and buried the box deep in the recesses of my intermittently malfunctioning mind. Other developments were, eh, developing. Wondrous, thrilling phenomena that had me in thrall. Poor excuse. I dragged grief for my father's too soon too sudden dying, acknowledged or not, into every new context, and everything was new. My grief was a pall on it all.

Discuss: What is the correct way to grieve? What were the other developments?

- I was always, from earliest memory, very quiet. My default was to watch and to listen, closely, attentively, instead of making noise. It's how I learned about everything. I never thought it was a weakness, but other people did—I was aloof, moody, sullen—and it did hold me back, and factored into needless conflict. I navigated life feeling fundamentally misunderstood, how adolescent! I pretend, people who know me, know different.

Action Item: It does not take very many words to make yourself understood. Use your words.

- I loved fiercely, guilelessly, for keeps. Hope against hope the people I loved felt it, generously. Discuss.

- Reviewing these Talking Points, I whiff mainly the sad funk of regret. And yes, the kids should know I was dealt an extra helping of remorse. Please tell them this, also: if I had it all to do again, that's a thing I would like to do. Maybe a bit better.

21. Valediction

Okay, so I don't know
the protocol here. I am
only trying to
stick the landing
in my way and
insofar as I am capable.

It was a
damn fine run
all things considered.
Sacred promises made
and mostly kept at least
for a good long while.
I bleed for those beautiful boys and
our fumbling, struggling, just us alone
fiercely steadfast our mission
to shape them into good men.

Swooping with Johnny, meekly dumb
an innocent apart, hauling a two ton chip
obvious even at a glance.
i remember the haircut, blouse
everyone grokked the million dollar smile
and i remember utter obliviousness.

How did I lose it that look
turning back at your
bedroom door in that
apartment on Elm Street,
dopey rapturous sweaty glowing,
if there was one moment
of revelation my essence distilled
fathomless radiance of knowing i was one
with you
never before never again
a foot above the Star parking lot
oblivious now halfway
home on the T.

A preposterous riddle, you had countless
causes for insult and profound fatigue
with the deafening silence
at the bottom of all those bottles;
with one too many hapless adventures
in magical thinking;
with, i mean really,
being yoked to a broken soul
capable only of spasmodic stretches
of being just barely normal.

There's more, always of course,

more and ever more
everything was forever
until it was no more
but sufficient unto the day
amen.

> *What ever dyes, was not mixt equally;*
> *If our two loves be one, or, thou and I*
> *Love so alike, that none doe slacken, none can die.*

Farewell and Godspeed.

(John Donne, "The Good-Morrow," 1633)